The Red Thread

The Red Thread

Nordic Design

Oak Publishing

Φ

The Red Thread

In the pale, pallid natural landscapes of Norway, Denmark, Sweden and Finland – the 'Nordic' region that this book addresses – the colour red stands out. This perhaps explains why the Swedish have an expression, *den röda tråden* (the red thread), which they use to describe the heart of the matter or the common denominator of something. The red thread is an essence that links together the soul of an experience, the narrative of a unified style or the collective heritage of many peoples. In some ways it can be used to describe the strangely forceful traits that unify four nations of separate histories, languages and cultures spread disparately across an unforgiving and vast terrain. In no other practice is this red thread brighter, tauter and more apparent than in Nordic design.

Functionality, simplicity, elegance and an emphasis on natural materials, the immediate signifiers of Nordic design are well known throughout the world. So too are many of its icons: the painted wooden Dala horses from Sweden, three-legged stools from Finland, Norwegian sheepskin rugs and myriad armchairs from Denmark. In the Nordic region, these designs are part of daily life. The 'red thread' these diverse, enduring objects share is that they are used democratically, they are designed to perform a function and are built to last. They also have the capacity to transcend genera-tions, style and fashion. This approach to design shapes entire Nordic cities: how the population builds and furnishes its homes and the way they interact with one another. It is both a philosophy for living and a way of life like no other region's on earth.

The Red Thread: Nordic Design explores this unique, all-encompassing approach in three chapters, inspired by the underlying significance of design in everyday life. The first, 'Design to Improve Spaces', celebrates the beauty, elegance and meticulously crafted features of the deep-rooted Nordic aesthetic that has become a global, cultural phenomenon. 'Design to Improve Life', meanwhile, focuses on the everyday – the modest, functional, accessible-to-all objects that are necessities for a practical lifestyle. The last, 'Design to Improve Relations', is where a sense of family, tradition, creativity and democratic values becomes the focus, in particular the understanding that Nordic design is built around human interaction.

One fundamental belief that reigns in Nordic countries is equality. From fjord to forest, these nations strive to even out the extremes of economic, social and cultural differences. Everyone, they believe, should have the same opportunities in education, health, career and housing. Imperatively, good design is also seen as a basic right: it is not necessarily fancy furniture or elite luxuries, but solid, sensible tools for living, including cutlery, cups, chairs or glassware. These objects are pieces of equipment made well and produced to last for generations. They are practical goods rather than 'design', which is why they are used as commonly in public spaces as they are in most homes. This egalitarian approach bridges the gap between private and public. There is little delineation made between domestic and social use: craft, longevity and simplicity are the democratic qualities that break down any environmental barriers.

Summers are bright and mild and spent out-doors in the Nordic region. Winters are harsh and largely lightless. Over centuries, homes in the region have been adapted to accom-modate both extremes. Dark seasons are spent with families and friends, huddled around oval dining tables (no 'heads of the table' here) and home-cooked food, with plenty of good conver-sation and room for both children and adults. It is simply a case of piling in and keeping warm, rendered in materials, layout and choice of furniture. In most Nordic homes birch furniture and paper-yarn rugs dominate, while stackable chairs and wall-hung bookcases combine to create a light and airy framework to see through these dark winter nights. Plenty of candles are a reminder that summer days will return, when the sun barely sets and activity is moved to wooden summerhouses by the waterside or on the forest's edge. The Nordic people are fundamentally an outdoors people who come alive in the summer. Even in its urban areas, one only need spend a summer's evening in the region to notice this: locals swim in the Stockholm archipelago, Helsinki outdoor swimming pools or sea baths in Copenhagen as though they were the Mediterranean.

The Nordic nations are vast and their populations small. With so much space, the landscape is intrinsic to the region's collective identity and has always been of huge significance, both as a playground and as a resource. These nations may be known today for high standards of living but historically they were not wealthy societies. People cultivated crops, gathered produce from the forests, caught fish and managed on whatever natural resources were available. This reliance on the land also had an integral effect on its design culture: if they built a house, it had to be able to stand for generations, and the furniture passed down with it. Personal possessions and decoration were minimal, therefore, a cherished cup, knife or blanket was an object for your children and grandchildren to inherit.

The Nordic design lauded today has its roots in this thrifty, austere approach. Furniture designers such as Alvar Aalto, Kaare Klint and Børge Mogensen all based their furniture on that of rural communities. They were inspired by the simplicity of objects found in farmhouses and ordinary homes and, rather than discard those chairs and tables that had functioned for hundreds of years, they improved and refined them

using the new techniques available at the start of the twentieth century. Nordic designers stuck with a simple palette of wood, clay, glass, leather, wool and textiles inspired by a domestic culture in which people made their houses and furniture out of whatever they could find.

Modern Nordic design is thus a continuation of this utilitarian ethic that has sometimes seemed at odds with currents in modern aesthetic thinking. Carl Malmsten's simple Lilla Åland chair [p.100], while inspired by a visit to the Finnström Church on Åland, is not so far removed from a seat you might have found on a Swedish farm in the mid-1800s. Marimekko's patterns [pp.155,173] recall traditional, rustic colour palettes, and raw wood remains untreated in much contemporary Nordic furniture, just as it did 100 years ago. A wealth of natural resources and a location slightly separate from the rest of central Europe helped foster a strong culture of craftsmanship, which has imbued Nordic design stylistically ever since. Handicrafts were made to be useful and long-lasting.

Yet Nordic design has never stood still. During the period immediately before and after World War II, designers began to experiment with groundbreaking methods. They discovered how to bend plywood, introduced machines into silver production, produced daring new lamp designs and sought out more unusual varieties of wood. New manufacturing techniques made it possible to lower production costs, and architects and designers across the region seized the opportunity to create exceptional designs that were also within reach of the average person. Finnish designer Alvar Aalto was hugely influential in the advancement of technical innovations in furniture making. His iconic Table 915 and Armchair 42 [pp.30,31], sculpted from laminated plywood, were extraordinary examples of the resilience, strength and beauty of such an apparently simple material.

It was at this point that the concept of 'Nordic design' began its gradual ascent to worldwide recognition. In the early twentieth century, Danish and Swedish Art Nouveau had made minor ripples abroad. In the interwar period, terms like 'Swedish Modern' were starting to be used, prompted by a display at the New York World's Fair in 1939. But it was following World War II that the region's design talent truly flourished. In the 1950s, a show entitled *Design in Scandinavia* spent three years touring twenty-four destinations across North America. This was followed by the *Arts of Denmark* exhibition, which was held at New York's Metropolitan Museum of Arts in 1960. It was little wonder that the world embraced Nordic design, for the democratic restraint of its vernacular style suited the post-war era as the world rebuilt itself. Crucially, its furniture industry managed to link industrial capabilities with craft traditions. It was a crowd-pleasing blend of man and machine: functional, but not too futuristic.

The Nordic nations soon realized that they could export their knowledge in addition to their furniture. In the early 1960s, for example, a group of Danes, Swedes and Finns travelled to Ireland to audit the nation's applied arts industry. Similar to their home countries, Ireland had a vast wealth of craft tradition in glass, pottery and textiles, yet had never succeeded in industrializing, much less sell it to the world like their Nordic counterparts had. The 'Scandinavian Design Group' published a lengthy report on lessons to be applied in a huge project that the design council of Ireland still benchmarks. The Nordic brand is built on the basic tenets of simplicity and timelessness, meaning it is easily adaptable to different cultures, climates and languages. In many ways, it is a universal rather than localized style: a simple, prototypical message that can be readily understood.

Nordic design is associated with clean, simple and elegant forms, natural material, tasteful colours and functionality – features that today remain sought-after around the world. But this approach extends far beyond the design world. From literature to food, lifestyle to fashion, cinema to architecture, the Nordic influence continues to be evident throughout contemporary culture. Within the past decade Nordic cuisine has gained a worldwide popularity for its understanding of traditional techniques and use of locally grown produce. Nordic noir crime fiction has captivated audiences within film, television and literature with its stark, cinematic landscapes and stylish interiors forming the backdrop to every scene, while urban planners from the region have inspired the way in which other countries develop their transport systems.

'Nordicness' is a global phenomenon but it is best experienced on a small scale in a Nordic home. Upon entering, visitors will be encouraged to take off their shoes – walking around in socks is perfectly natural in the relaxed atmosphere of a Nordic home. It is born out of etiquette, but social equality too; Nordic nationals do not – quite literally – stand on ceremony. They will be immediately welcomed with an elderflower *saft* in Aino Aalto glassware [pp. 182–3], offered a seat on the Poul Kjærholm chair [p. 20] and encouraged to take a look around.

From the Vipp pedal bins in the kitchen [p. 238] to the the Arne Jacobsen Series 7 chairs around the dining table [p. 39], from the Pia Wallen slippers next to the bed [p. 228] to the Fiskars scissors in the dresser drawer [p. 154]: it is easy to feel a sense of déjà vu in a Nordic home. They are, to put it bluntly, uncannily similar.

It begins in the very foundations of Nordic home building. Prefabricated housing has been quintessential in the region since the Industrial Revolution, when the idea of mobile, mass-produced housing was first dreamed up, with plenty of wood and sawmills able to carry out production at an unprecedented pace. Housing shortages after World War II augmented its popularity, with both Arne Jacobsen and Alvar Alto conceptualizing 'catalogue' homes.

Yet today there remains a strong self-build culture too: witness the many rustic A-frame summerhouses by the lakes of Finland or on the Swedish archipelago. In both architecture and design, there is a dichotomy between the equal popularity of the handcrafted and the mass-produced. Nordic interiors are a mix of aesthetics tempered by good common sense and, in many homes, cultish staples of vernacular, factory-made design will sit alongside highly personal craft objects.

The value placed on craft and how things are made still resonates today. The use-and-discard mentality has never taken hold in the Nordic design tradition (even Ikea is now investing in repair and re-use services). The more things are used, the more beautiful they become. The success of 2nd Cycle, a store in Helsinki that sells second-hand Artek furniture, is testament to this. This is not nostalgia, it is seen as an 'environmental strategy'. Nordic designers and architects have become world leaders in sustainability. Although this has grown to encompass zero carbon emissions and green approaches to the built environment, it has its roots in this belief in using what already exists.

This merging of old and new, handicrafts and industrial design, function and beauty, forms the most characterized facet of a Nordic home: the elusive cosiness – known as *hygge* in Denmark, *mys* in Sweden, *kose* in Norway and *lämpöä* in Finland. Cosiness is brought to life in the fabric of any home there. Tealights glow on every surface; windowsills are deep (thick walls are naturally essential in the cold climate); furniture

hovers above the floor; and pendant lights dangle above dining tables at eye height (the rule of thumb in Denmark is 60 cm/24 in above a surface). The Nordic countries are blessed with endless forests, meaning every home is alive with combinations of warming, tactile oak, birch, beech and ash. Reindeer hides [p. 27] or sheepskin rugs are never far away during the winter months. This is why, fundamentally, they are such pleasant spaces to spend time in. It is why they are built for social interaction, designed for all seasons and for all people, held together by a single red thread.

Design to
Improve Spaces

As many will testify, the Nordic aesthetic is synonymous with timeless simplicity, considered minimalism and a focus on natural materials, quality and functionality. While these characteristics can be identified in many aspects of contemporary Nordic culture, it is through design that they become most explicitly apparent. From everyday domestic items to exquisitely produced decorative glassware, and from traditional handmade textiles to mass-produced objects found in homes across the globe, the Nordic trademarks are inherent in almost everything.

Yet it would be misleading to say that this results in a one-size-fits-all approach to design – personality and innovation are never far away. In fact, it is in the celebration of contrast that true Nordic design is revealed, particularly within a domestic setting. These are places where wood is boldly combined with marble, slate, leather, wicker, glass, metal and textiles. A fabric sofa contrasts with a marble-topped coffee table, a leather armchair complements an oiled-oak bookshelf. Nordic interiors expertly combine surfaces, textures and materials to create a kind of gentle friction, an environment that is both dynamic and harmonious.

Making a home is about mixing not only materials, but also the old and the new, commonplace items with high-end designer pieces. Once a relatively poor set of nations, the Nordic region has always placed enormous value on how things are made, where things come from and on things that are built to last. Qualities that were once a necessity are still evident today in how people occupy their homes, even though the need for them may no longer be as vital. Regardless of passing trends or changes in personal economic status, Nordic interiors and the objects contained within them do not actually change that much. Browse through any second-hand furniture store in the region and you will see why good-quality furniture is held onto for so long. Retaining a sense of familiarity is what gives homes a soul, comfort and security.

The Nordic interest in holding onto good things and passing on heirlooms is explained, in part, by practicality, not necessarily sentimentality. Things are kept because they are useful and, although there are exceptions, the rest is largely jettisoned. A Nordic home must have a sense of clarity; there should be space between the furniture as well as underneath it; walls are often left bare and, even when more furniture could be squeezed in, restraint is practised. Rather a few good pieces than many mediocre ones.

Bearing this functional rigour in mind, however, it would be incorrect to assume that Nordic interiors are lacking in character. Undercurrents of joy, playfulness and imagination are subtly imbued throughout the home. One of the best ways to understand this balance between style and function is through an exploration into humble Nordic armchair. Throughout the twentieth century, furniture designers refined the classic styles of chair until the designs became so optimal that they gained international recognition and success, embodying Nordic design on a global scale, as they still do today. What appealed to the world, at first glance, were their simplicity, comfort and elegance. Designs like Bruno Mathsson's Eva lounge chair [p. 88] and Kaare Klint's Safari Chair [p. 35] are fundamentally utilitarian, pieces stripped back to only the elements needed for a place to sit down. Yet take a closer look and before long you will notice the sculptural, almost flamboyant, details present in other designs: the gently curving wings of Arne Jacobsen's Swan chair [p. 21]; the anthropomorphism of the Pelican Chair by Finn Juhl [p. 72]; or the fanned-out plumage of Hans Wegner's spoke-back Peacock chair [p. 129]. Though a great deal of

Nordic design is considered to be minimalist, there is a huge amount of character and fun evident in it too. What Nordic designers have never permitted is for their creative vision to get in the way of functionality. They welcome design objects that elevate a space and give it an extra aesthetic dimension, but not those that are so overtly stylized that their usefulness is compromised. Juhl's Pelican Chairs are some of the most sculptural seats in Danish design history but, above all, they remain armchairs intended to fill the need of sitting back with a good book and a cup of coffee within arm's reach.

In the Nordic region, functionalism is a basic requirement for what people keep in their homes, but as these armchairs demonstrate, this is not necessarily at the expense of beauty and imagination. Contrary to popular belief, design for design's sake is occasionally allowed – the concept that 'beautiful things make your life better' is still highly regarded in the region. This is especially true in the applied arts and has always been prevalent in the rich tradition of pottery and glassware. Sophisticated and expertly crafted pieces such as the Kraka vase [p. 96] by Swedish glass artist Sven Palmqvist or the contemporary ceramic collections of Tortus Copenhagen [p. 89] serve little function other than being decorative – they have been designed with the purpose of bringing a sense of style to an interior. But they also have the capacity to bring happiness too, derived from an understanding of the expert craft that went into making them, whether on the potter's wheel or in the hands of a glassblower.

Character, colour and creative flair are present in many aspects of Nordic design, especially in circumstances where designers turn to nature for inspiration. It is apparent in the way Jacobsen, Juhl and Wegner were all inspired by ornithology when designing their armchairs; it is evident in the floral patterns of Arabia pottery [pp. 122–3] or Oiva Toikka's ornamental glass birds [p. 51], each with their own distinct personality; in the lively, vibrant textile designs of Josef Frank [pp. 70–71, 84] and Marie Gudme Leth [p. 101]. It is the combination of all these things – glass, furniture, ceramics, textiles and art – that gives a Nordic home its ambience. Of course, the building's architectural framework and its inhabitants also contribute to its atmosphere, but it is the furniture and the way that a house is 'styled' that really make a home.

Nordic design is conceived to be used, but some pieces also provide a framework for the way they should be used. If you were to place an Ox chair [pp. 32–33] by Danish designer Hans Wegner in a living room, for example, you would discover that it takes on a sculptural role in the interior design. Its very definite shape commands the space, meaning that it cannot be combined with just anything. A similar effect can be seen with Poul M Volther's Corona chair [p. 52] or one of Grete Jalk's origami-like ply-wood seats [p. 49]. These are pieces with such a strong individual expression that they are best placed together with objects of the same calibre. But as well as being objects to admire, they also represent an invitation to be used, and if they are successful in their intentions, they have the ability to liberate the user: once the armchair or dining table has been placed in position, it does not need to be thought of again.

Fundamentally, there are no rules in Nordic spaces; there are just systems and beliefs that date back centuries to when homes were a refuge away from the harsh landscape outside. They were places to sleep, shelter and seek some comfort, but they were also places of contentment. Emphasis was placed on sour-cing enjoyment from craft, nature, colour and company. This is deeply rooted in what Nordic homes were filled with and, crucially, how they are experienced, even today.

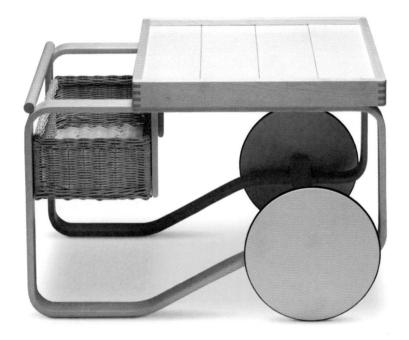

↑   Tea Trolley 901, Alvar Aalto, Artek, 1936
→   Drop chairs, Arne Jacobsen, Fritz Hansen, 1958

← Fionia Stool, Jens Quistgaard, Skagerak, 1962
↑ Copenhagen Collection, OeO Studio, Kohchosai Kosuga, 2016

↑   PK22 lounge chair, Poul Kjærholm, Ejvind Kold Christensen, 1956 / Currently manufactured by Fritz Hansen
→   Swan chair, Arne Jacobsen, Fritz Hansen, 1958

←   Dancing Dune collection, Anna Elzer Oscarson, AEO, 2016
↑   539 stool, Hans Wegner, Johannes Hansen, 1950s
⇉   Grand Prix chairs, Arne Jacobsen, Fritz Hansen, 1957 / Super-Elliptical table, Piet Hein and Bruno Mathsson, 1964

<< Georg Stool, Console Table and Table Mirror, Chris Liljenberg Halstrøm, Skagerak, 2012
↑ Armchair 400, Alvar Aalto, Artek, 1936

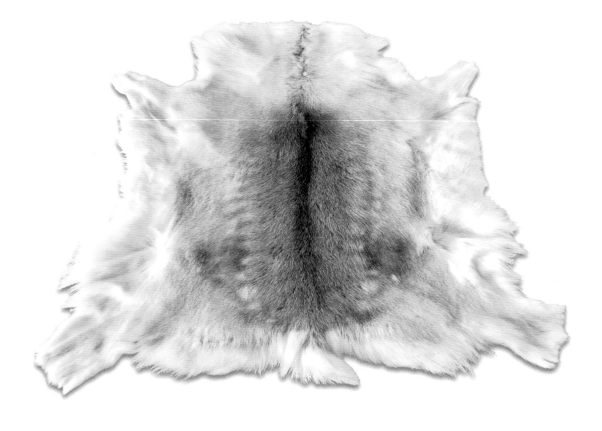

↑   Reindeer hide
⇝   Provence Bowl, Per Lütken, Holmegaard, 1955

<<   Spanish Chair, Børge Mogensen, Fredericia, 1958
↑   Table 915, Alvar Aalto, Artek, 1932
→   Armchair 42, Alvar Aalto, Artek, 1932 / Pendant Lights TW003, Tapio Wirkkala, 1960

« Ox chairs and footstool, Hans Wegner, AP Stolen, 1960 / Currently manufactured by Erik Jørgensen / Insula table,
    Ernst & Jensen, Erik Jørgensen, 2009; AJ Table lamp, Arne Jacobsen, Louis Poulsen, 1960
↑ Church Chair, Kaare Klint, Fritz Hansen, 1936 / Currently manufactured by dk3
→ Safari Chair and Stool, Kaare Klint, Carl Hansen & Søn, 1933

↑   PK24 chaise longue, Poul Kjærholm, Ejvind Kold Christensen, 1965 / Currently manufactured by Fritz Hansen
→   Kubus 4 candle holder, Mogens Lassen, by Lassen, 1962 / Kubus bowl, by Lassen, 2009
↠   Hallingdal 65 textile, Nanna Ditzel, Kvadrat, 1965

<< Series 7 chairs, Arne Jacobsen, Fritz Hansen, 1955 / Circular Table, Arne Jacobsen, 1968
↑ Dot stools, Arne Jacobsen, Fritz Hansen, 1954
→ Harp Chair, Jørgen Høvelskov, Christensen & Larsen Møbelhåndværk, 1968 / Currently manufactured by Koch Design

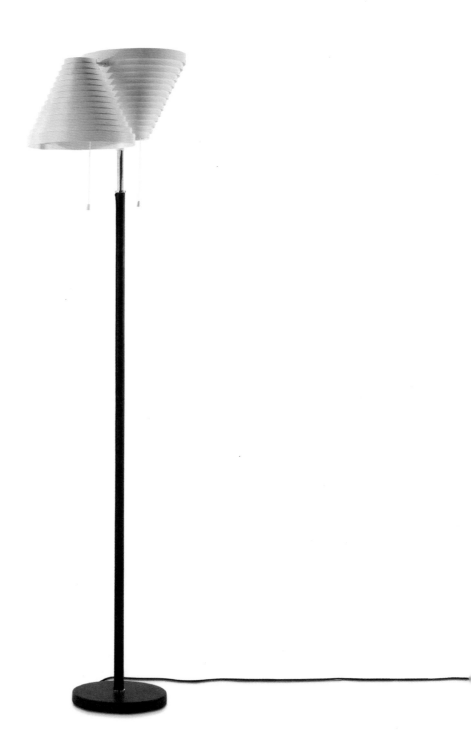

↑   Floor Light A810, Alvar Aalto, Artek, 1959

↑ Poäng chair, Noboru Nakamura, Ikea, 1976

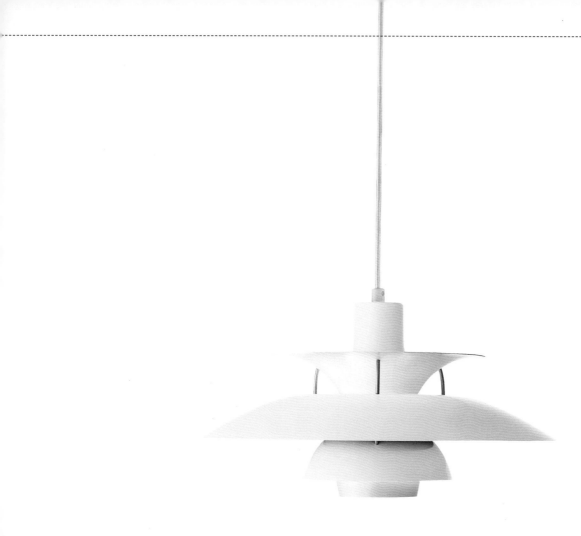

↑   PH50 lamp, Poul Henningsen, Louis Poulsen, 1958
→   Ant chairs, Arne Jacobsen, Fritz Hansen, 1952 / Coffee table, Arne Jacobsen, 1968; Kaiser Idell Pendant, Christian Dell, 1931

↑   Aksla armchair, Gerhard Berg, Stokke, 1960

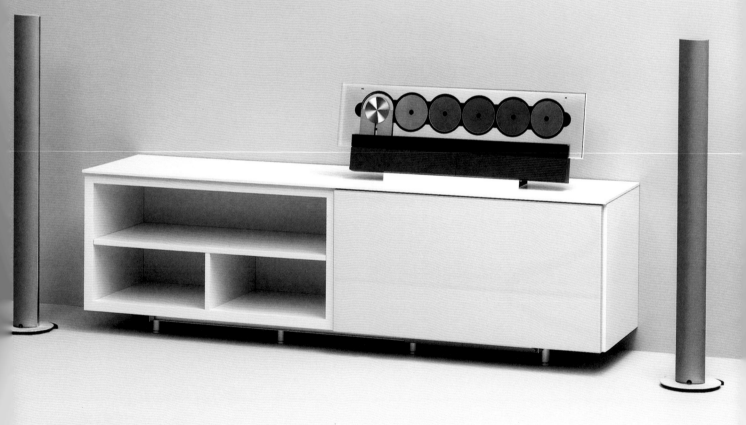

↑   BeoSound 9000, David Lewis, Bang & Olufsen, 1996

↑   Block Lamp, Harri Koskinen, Design House Stockholm, 1996
→   GJ Chair and Nesting Tables, Grete Jalk, Poul Jeppesen, 1963 / Currently manufactured by Lange Production

↑   Chanterelle vase, Tapio Wirkkala, Iittala, 1946
→   Birds, Oiva Toikka, Iittala, 1972

←   Corona Chair, Poul M Volther, Erik Jørgensen, 1964
↑   Reclining lounge chair, Bendt Winge, Bjarne Hansen, 1958

↑   Spoke-Back Sofa, Børge Mogensen, Fredericia, 1945
→   Le Klint 101 (The Lantern), Kaare Klint, Le Klint, 1943
↠   Woven rugs, Sofia Carlson and Lotta Ågerup, Swedish Rags, 2015

« Hanging Egg Chair, Nanna and Jørgen Ditzel, R Wengler, 1957 / Currently manufactured by Sika Design
↑ Fuga bowls, Sven Palmqvist, Orrefors, 1954

Bolle, Tapio Wirkkala, Venini, 1966

↑   Slateplate series, Gurli Elbækgaard, 2014

↑   High Stools, Space Copenhagen, Mater, 2009

←   Shell Chairs CH07, Hans Wegner, Carl Hansen & Søn, 1963
↑   Turning Trays, Finn Juhl, Torben Ørskov, 1956 / Currently manufactured by Architectmade

← Another Rug, All The Way To Paris, &Tradition, 2014
↑ Lantern candle holders, Harri Koskinen, Iittala, 1999

← Brass vase collection, Pierre Forsel, Skultuna, 1950s
↑ Birds, Kristian Vedel, Torben Ørskov, 1959 / Currently manufactured by Architectmade

↑   Lune Lamp, Sverre Uhnger, Brdr. Krüger, 2014
→   Unfold lamp, Form Us With Love, Muuto, 2010
↠   Print collection, Josef Frank, Svenskt Tenn, 2015

↑   Pelican Chair, Finn Juhl, Niels Vodder, 1940 / Currently manufactured by Onecollection
→   Nyhavn Dining Table, Finn Juhl, Bovirke, 1953 / Currently manufactured by Onecollection / Reading Chairs, Finn Juhl, 1953;
    Glove Cabinet, Finn Juhl, 1961

← Gräshoppa Floor Lamp, Greta Magnusson Grossman, Bergboms, 1947 / Currently manufactured by Gubi / Grand Piano Sofa, Gubi Olsen, 1982
↑ The Flag Halyard Chair, Hans Wegner, Getama, 1950 / Currently manufactured by PP Møbler

↑   PK91 folding stool, Poul Kjærholm, Ejvind Kold Christensen, 1961 / Currently manufactured by Fritz Hansen
→   Propeller Stool, Kaare Klint, Carl Hansen & Søn, 1930

↑   45 Chair, Finn Juhl, Niels Vodder, 1945 / Currently manufactured by Onecollection
→   Stool ML42, Mogens Lassen, by Lassen, 1942

↑ Topan Pendant, Verner Panton, Louis Poulsen, 1959 / Currently manufactured by &Tradition

↑   Kevi office chair, Jørgen Rasmussen, Kevi A/S, 1973 / Currently manufactured by Engelbrechts

← Sideboard with Tray Unit, Finn Juhl, Bovirke, 1955 / Currently manufactured by Onecollection
↑ Kivi Votive candle holders, Heikki Orvola, Iittala, 1988 / Alvar Aalto Collection Votives, Pentagon Design, 2006
↠ Under Ekvatorn (Under the Equator) print, Josef Frank, Svenskt Tenn, 1941

<< PH 3½ - 2½ Table lamp, Poul Henningsen, Louis Poulsen, 1926 / Colonial Chair, Ole Wanscher, Carl Hansen & Søn, 1949
↑ Apple vase, Ingeborg Lundin, Orrefors, 1955

↑　The Woods, Andreas Engesvik, StokkeAustad, 2013

↑   Eva lounge chair, Bruno Mathsson, Bruno Mathsson International, 1933
→   Unika collection, Eric Landon, Tortus Copenhagen, 2016
⇢   Royal System, Poul Cadovius, Cado, 1948 / Currently manufactured by dk3 / Copilot Chair, Asger Soelberg, 2010

↑   Ovalis vases, Tapio Wirkkala, Iittala, 1958

↑   Papa Bear Chair, Hans Wegner, AP Stolen, 1951 / Currently manufactured by PP Møbler
⇒   AJ Table lamp, Arne Jacobsen, Louis Poulsen, 1960

«   The Tired Man easy chair, Flemming Lassen, by Lassen, 1935 / Twin Table 42, by Lassen, 2015

↑   Kraka vase, Sven Palmqvist, Orrefors, 1944

↑   Rang Side Table, StokkeAustad, Tonning & Stryn, 2015
↦   Flower Pot pendant, Verner Panton, Louis Poulsen, 1968 / Currently manufactured by &Tradition

« Aalto Vase, Alvar Aalto, Iittala, 1937 / Stool 60, Alvar Aalto, Artek, 1933
↑ Lilla Åland chair, Carl Malmsten, Stolab, 1942
→ Kirsebær (Cherry) print, Marie Gudme Leth, Dansk Kattuntrykkeri, 1946

↑   K-7017 vase, Severin Brørby, Hadeland Glassverk, c.1960

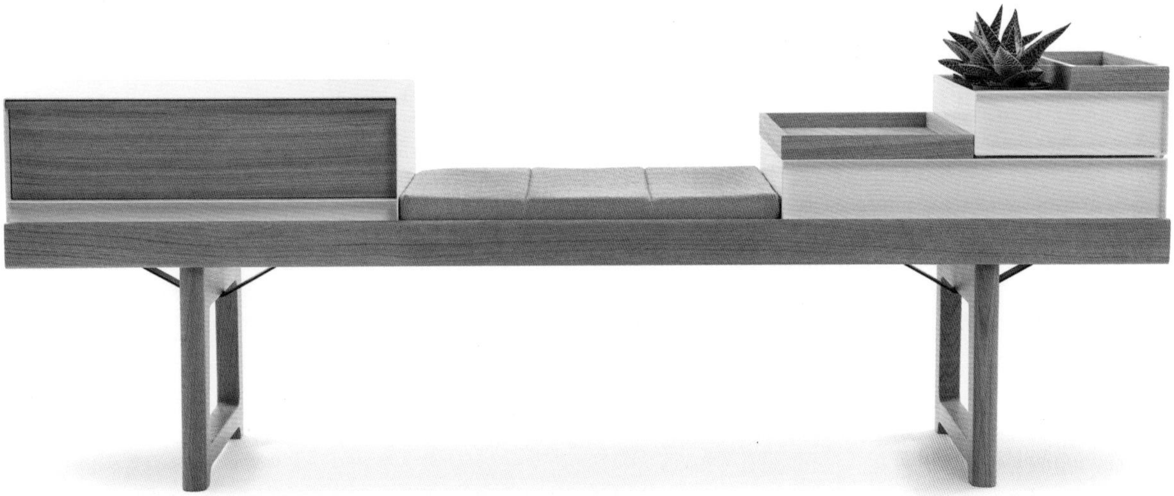

↑ Krobo Accessories (Frame, Trays, Cushion, Drawer), Anderssen & Voll, FjordFiesta, 2014 (re-issue) / Original design by Torbjørn Afdal, 1960
→› High Chairs K65, Alvar Aalto, Artek, 1935 / Semi Pendant lamps, Bonderup & Thorup, Gubi, 1968

←← Wishbone Chair CH24, Hans Wegner, Carl Hansen & Søn, 1949
← Valet Chair, Hans Wegner, Johannes Hansen, 1953 / Currently manufactured by PP Møbler
↑ HK Pitcher, Henning Koppel, Georg Jensen, 1952

« Tableware, KH Würtz, 2006
↑ Bowl, Timo Sarpaneva, Iittala, 1958

↑   512 folding chairs, Hans Wegner, Johannes Hansen, 1949 / Currently manufactured by PP Møbler

↑ Festivo candle holders, Timo Sarpaneva, Iittala, 1966

↑   Rattan table, Bjørn Engø, John Sæther, c.1951

↑   Åttebladrose Red Table Runner, Ekelund, 1997

↑   Bachelor chair and table, Verner Panton, Montana, 1955

↑   Winston armchair, Torbjørn Afdal, Nesjestranda Møbelfabrikk, c.1961

↑   Ericofon (Cobra Phone), Gösta Thames, Ralph Lysell and Hugo Blomberg, Ericsson, 1954

117

↑   Conform coffee table, Herman Bongard, Plus, 1961

↑   Rosewood wine rack, Torsten Johansson, Ab Formträ, 1960

← Nomad Chair, Sebastian Jørgensen, We Do Wood, 2015
↑ Stoneware vase, Svend Hammershøi, Herman A Kähler, 1930s

↑ Valencia collection, Ulla Procopé, Arabia, 1960

↑   Vase with hare's fur glaze, Berndt Friberg, Gustavsberg, 1962

↑   Glass vases, Benny Motzfeld, Plus, 1971

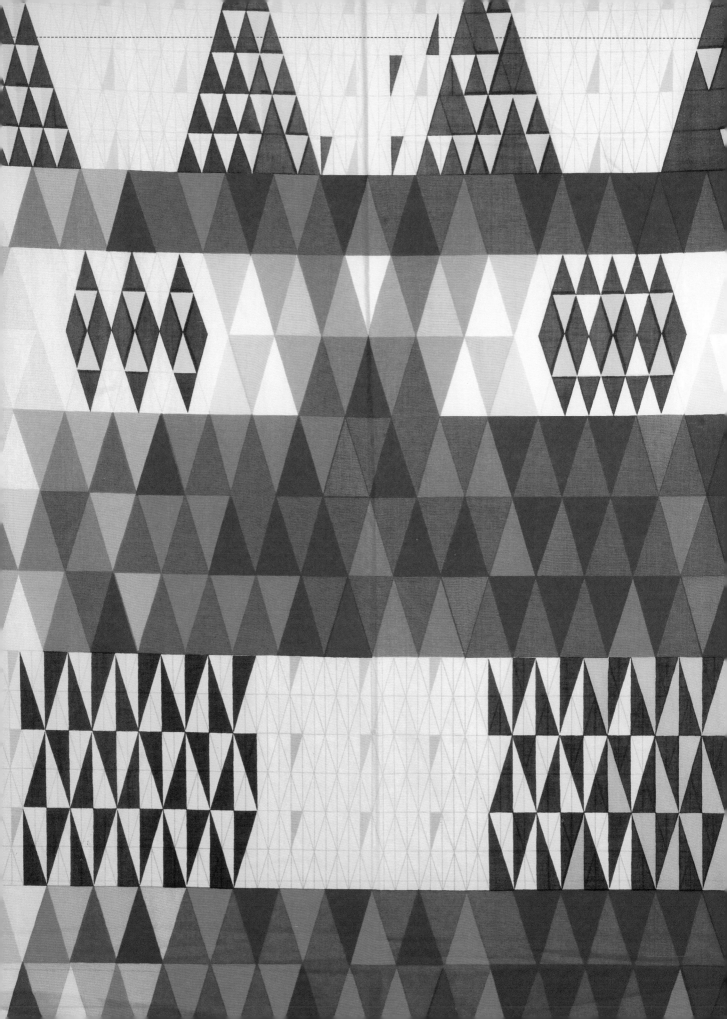

← Pythagoras print, Sven Markelius, Ljungbergs, 1952 / Currently manufactured by Bemz
↑ Tale stool, Ilmari Tapiovaara, Asko, 1953

↑   Chair, Magnus Læssøe Stephensen, AJ Iversen, 1940
→   Peacock chair, Hans Wegner, Johannes Hansen, 1947 / Currently manufactured by PP Møbler / PH 3½ - 2½ Table lamp,
    Poul Henningsen, Louis Poulsen, 1926

↑ Glass vase, Benny Motzfeldt, Plus, 1970
→ Ballroom pendant lamps, Design by Us, 2013 / Wire Basket, Ferm Living, 2013

↑   Pollo vase, Tapio Wirkkala, Rosenthal, 1970

↑   Ball Chair, Eero Aarnio, Asko, 1963 / Currently manufactured by Adelta

↑   Pop glasses, Gunnar Cyren, Orrefors, 1967

↑   Morris tables, Kirsi Gullichsen, Habitek, 2010

↑ Slipgraal bowl, Edward Hald, Orrefors, c.1950

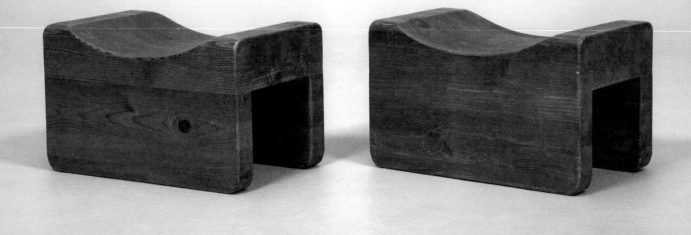

↑   Utö stools, Axel Einar Hjorth, Nordiska Kompaniet, 1930

↑   Panton Chairs, Verner Panton, Vitra, 1960

↑   Mademoiselle Lounge Chairs, Ilmari Tapiovaara, Artek, 1956
↠   Semi Pendant, Bonderup & Thorup, Gubi, 1968 / Gubi 1F chairs, Komplot Design, 2003; Gubi dining table, Komplot Design, 2013

↞   Egg chair, Arne Jacobsen, Fritz Hansen, 1957
↑   Blåarp rug, Barbro Nilsson, Märta Måås-Fjetterström AB, 1962

↑   Screen 100, Alvar Aalto, Artek, 1936

Design to
Improve Life

Open a kitchen drawer in almost any Danish home and there will likely be a small, steel tin opener [p. 163] by the centuries-old utensil maker Raadvad. Despite it being the creation of Jens Quistgaard, one of Nordic design's most important figures, few people would consider the elegant 'Shark Fin' a designer object. It is a humble and unassuming item, a simple, flat metal surface with a rising lip at one side – the 'fin' that gives it its name – and designed with one purpose in mind: to open tinned goods. However, this is not to say that Quistgaard paid no regard to its aesthetic potential; even though the design is democratic in nature and intended for daily use, it has not been stripped of all its beauty.

Much like a pair of orange Fiskars scissors [p. 154] from Finland, a set of Gense cutlery [p. 164] from Sweden or a Bjørklund cheese knife [p. 174] from Norway, Quistgaard's tin opener represents a common thread in Nordic design: it owes its existence to a designer aiming to solve a problem or make a specific chore easier. It was created to be used day in, day out in the household – not meant to be especially decorative or status-defining, but still a thing of understated elegance.

Whether Nordic designers sit down to work on a thermos flask, a set of cutlery or a frying pan, they will likely approach the task with the same degree of seriousness they would bring to designing a motorway overpass. Every single detail is considered and many different solutions are tested; the Nordic designer's common mission is to investigate how to make an object as streamlined, safe and user-friendly as possible. And by constantly tightening up the materials and dropping all unnecessary decoration, the designer navigates his or her way to an object that is universally useful and that, as a reflection of its fitness for purpose, might also be seen as beautiful. Nordic designers

seize everyday challenges and offer solutions that make life better for ordinary households. Pans are designed that are easy to clean and that conduct the heat optimally when they are placed on the hob. Decoration is removed from cutlery, so that focus is shifted from the utensil to the food that it handles. Tea towels, woven from the best cotton, are often so hard-wearing that they last many years.

Contemporary Nordic design is also founded on these timeless principles of simplicity and practicality. Brands such as Design House Stockholm, Normann Copenhagen and Ikea are all exemplary in investigating the boundaries between pared-back, utilitarian design and pieces that meet the demands of a global consumer who seeks style as well as functionality. It is a fine line to walk, but it is conceivable to imagine that a handful of their creations could exist in fifty years time, without seeming dated, and still prove to be as useful as ever.

This intention extends to electronics too, in particular to the hardware made by Danish company Bang & Olufsen [pp. 227, 233, 235]. Founded in 1925, it made its name producing portable radios. The company's design strategy was built on clean, simple and intuitive forms, an approach that is largely credited to Jacob Jensen, whose collaboration with Bang & Olufsen spanned almost three decades. Their significant contribution to the world of audio equipment culminated in the exhibition *Bang & Olufsen: Design for Sound by Jacob Jensen*, at the Museum of Modern Art, New York in 1978. The curator at the time described how the thirty-four pieces in the show – including turntables, telephones, radio sets and televisions – were united in being 'beautiful objects in their own right that do not inordinately call attention to themselves'. This ethos remains the case today, and has arguably set a precedent for the rational, highly pared-back design adopted by contemporary electronics manufacturers around the world.

Such design principles are rooted far back in the cultural history and craft traditions of the Nordic region. The present goes hand in hand with the past, and a connection with very early folk culture is evident in most modern homes in the basic utensils that have been used for generations, such as rolling pins [p. 218], chopping boards [p. 197] and butter knives [p. 190]. This faith in the timeless usefulness of certain things, if made well, also extends beyond ephemera. These objects, for example, carry with them notions of simplicity in eating too.

Although there has been a huge revolution in Nordic cuisine in recent years, much of the fare enjoyed today owes its heritage to traditional recipes and cooking methods. In Sweden it is known as *husmankost* (farmer's food), and consists of wholesome, hearty dishes made with locally-sourced produce. Across the Nordic region, such recipes are handed down through generations, based on age-old techniques of cooking, curing, preserving and baking. Entertaining is arguably 'traditional' too: the trend for informal, communal dining, evident in world-class restaurants in Nordic cities, stretches back to simpler times when people would gather together around one table to share a meal with friends and family. However avant-garde gastronomy and dining have become in the region, their roots are firmly in the past – just like the cutlery that is used during meals or the utensils required for their preparation.

Nordic people understand that a good piece of design, if taken care of, will in all likelihood be an object that will be kept for life. Indeed, such an investment often comes at a price. What can appear at first to be a large cost is justifiable when a piece is of good quality since it is, in

effect, the beginning of a long-term relationship. If you choose well, there is an everlasting reward – both aesthetic and functional – which outweighs the financial cost. When something lasts, and is handed down through generations, it acquires a patina of age, its own anthology of stories and understandably becomes sentimentalized. Glassware, tablecloths, kitchen utensils and sets of crockery all become part of a story that is imparted and retold: about how the piece was crafted, why it was made that way, and why and when its owner bought it.

Nordic design is about history, about the Nordic populations' perception of themselves as strong design nations. It is a cultural identity that stretches far back in history, pre-dating the Industrial Revolution. And while this outlook is first and foremost about function and creating things that make everyday life easier, it is also about aesthetics and a belief that the everyday is best filled with a thousand small treasures. Even if it is simply a tin opener in the kitchen drawer.

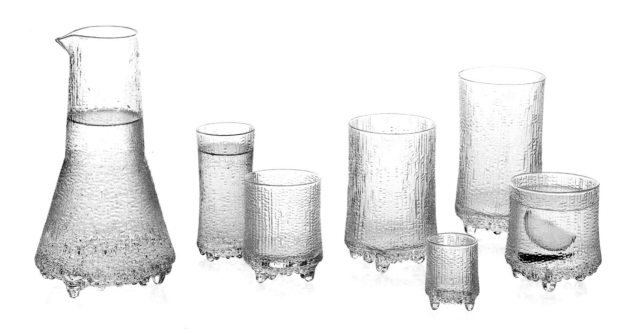

↑   Ultima Thule glassware, Tapio Wirkkala, Iittala, 1968

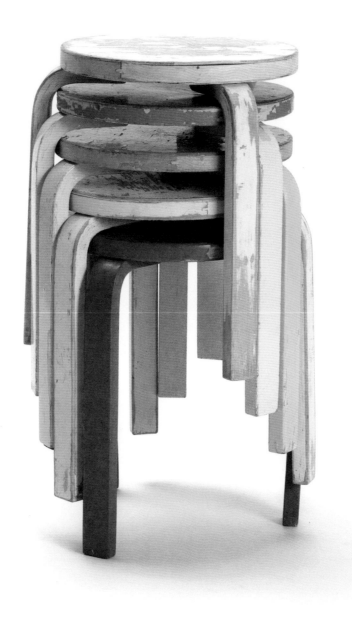

↑   Stool 60, Alvar Aalto, Artek, 1933

↑   Thermodan coffee set, Axel Brüel, Lyngby Porcelæn, 1957
→   Blue Fluted Plain Porcelain Set, Arnold Krog (1880s re-design), Royal Copenhagen, 1775

←   Teema bowl and plate, Kaj Franck, Arabia, 1952 / Currently manufactured by Iittala / Kartio pitcher, Kaj Franck, 1958;
     Essence wine glass, Alfredo Häberli, 2001
↑   Lion cutlery, Bertel Gardberg, Hackman, 1958

↑   O-Series Scissors, Olof Bäckström, Fiskars, 1961
→   Tiara collection, Erja Hirvi, Marimekko, 2016

↑ Turn Around juicer, Kibisi, Muuto, 2013

↑ Pepper mills, Jens Quistgaard, Dansk, 1960s

← Rewrite desk, GamFratesi, Ligne Roset, 2011 / TV chair, Pierre Paulin, 1953
↑ Fjord flatware, Jens Quistgaard, Dansk, c.1950

↑   Cylinda-Line, Arne Jacobsen, Stelton, 1967

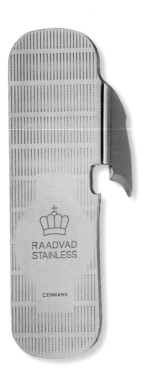

↑   Focus de Luxe cutlery, Folke Arström, Gense, 1955
→   Corky carafe and glasses, Andreas Engesvik, Muuto, 2011

← Focus floor screen, Note Design Studio, Zilenzio, 2016 / Drop chairs, Arne Jacobsen, Fritz Hansen, 1958
↑ Tapio glass, Tapio Wirkkala, Iittala, 1952

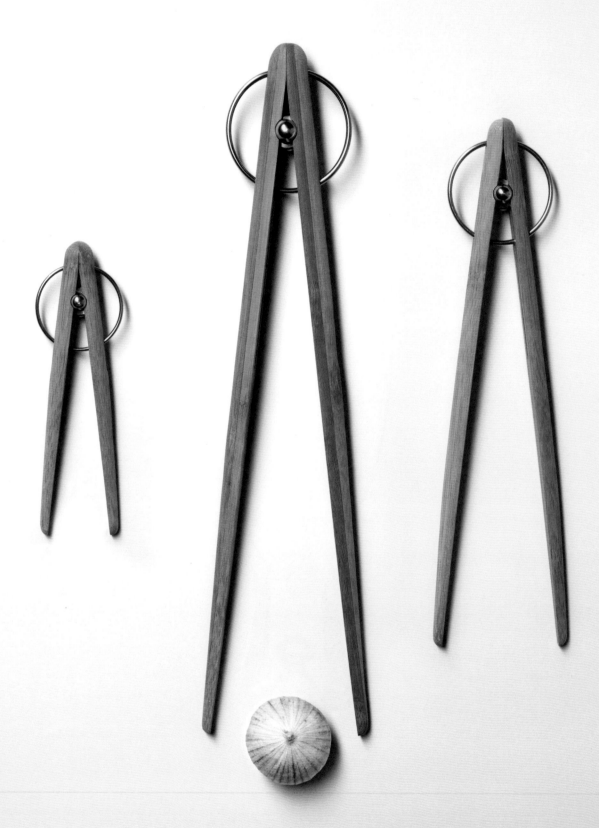

↑   Pick Up tongs, Stig Ahlstrom, Design House Stockholm, 2001

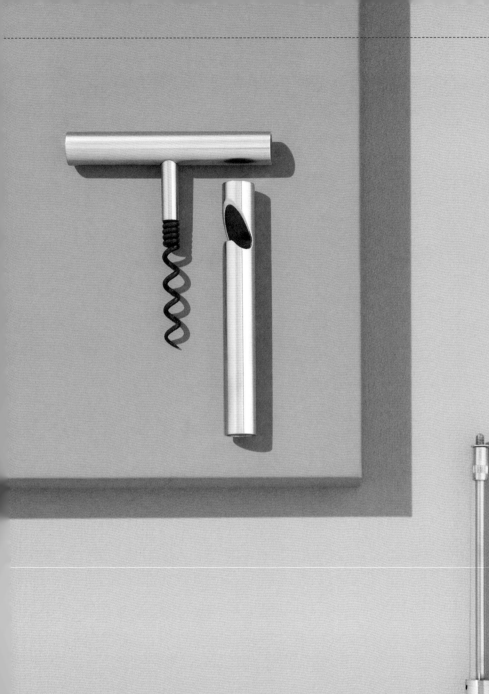

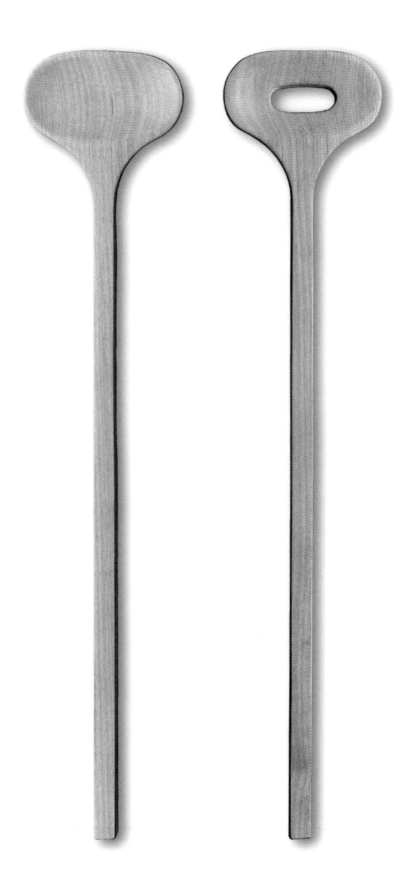

↑   Salad Servers, Carina Seth Andersson, Iittala, 1998
→   AGA cooker, Gustaf Dalén, AGA, 1922 / Currently manufactured by AGA Rangemaster Ltd

↑   Sarpaneva cast-iron pot, Timo Sarpaneva, Rosenlew & Co., 1960 / Currently manufactured by Iittala
→   Unikko print, Maija Isola, Marimekko, 1964

↑   Frigi refrigerator storage jars, Gunnar Nylund, Rörstrand, 1941

↑ Nya Clara can opener, Sigvard Bernadotte, Nils Johan, 1963

↑   1718 stacking glasses and 1618 pitcher, Saara Hopea-Untracht, Nuutajärvi, 1954

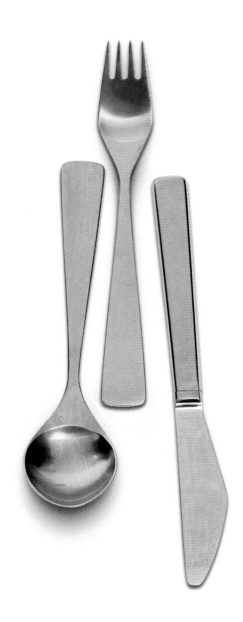

↑   Maya cutlery, Tias Eckhoff, Norsk Stalpress, 1961 / Currently manufactured by Stelton
→   Kastehelmi (Dewdrop) collection, Oiva Toikka, Iittala, 1964

↑ Picnic Set, Sigvard Bernadotte, Husqvarna, 1959

↑   Washing-up Bowl and Brush, Ole Jensen, Normann Copenhagen, 1996

↑ Pressed glass collection, Aino Aalto, Karhula, 1932 / Currently manufactured by Iittala

↑   Salt and Pepper Shakers, Arne Korsmo, J Tostrup, 1945

↑ Winston collection, Per Lütken, Holmegaard, 1956

↑   Classic peeler, Raadvad, 1924

↑ Chambourd coffee maker, Bodum, 1950s
↠ Kobenstyle enamelware, Jens Quistgaard, Dansk, 1956

↑   Butter knife, Thure Permansson, 1960s

↑   Leaf dishes, Tapio Wirkkala, Martti Lindqvist, c.1951

↑   Waffle Iron, Skeppshult, 1906

↑   Wooden ladle

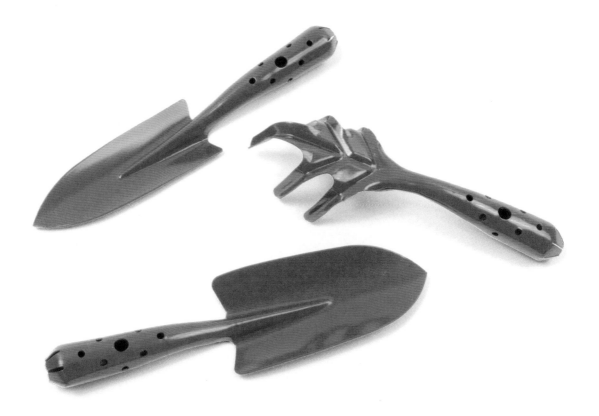

↑   Garden Tool Set, Nyby, 1976
→   Good Morning moka pot and Tuamotu hob, Anderssen & Voll, 2012

↑ OLE collection, Ole Jensen, Royal Copenhagen, 1997

↑   Cutting boards, Morten Høeg-Larsen, Sløjd, 2012
»   Margrethe mixing bowls, Sigvard Bernadotte and Acton Bjørn, Rosti Mepal, 1950

↑   Handmade potato masher, John Piippo, date unknown

↑   Ice bucket, Magnus Stephensen, Georg Jensen, 1951
»   Viktigt carafe and glass, Ingegerd Råman, Ikea, 2016

« Karui Trays, GamFratesi, Skultuna, 2015
← Emma electric kettles, HolmbäckNordentoft, Stelton, 2015
↑ Restore basket, Mika Tolvanen, Muuto, 2009

← Sauna bucket
↑ Tools 5L casserole pan, Björn Dahlström, Iittala, 1998

↑   Tea service, Gertrud Vasegaard, Bing & Grondahl, 1956

↑   Terma frying pan, Stig Lindberg, Gustavsberg, 1955
↠   AJ Cutlery, Arne Jacobsen, Georg Jensen, 1957

<< EM77 Vacuum Jug, Erik Magnussen, Stelton, 1977 / Theo Milk Jug and Mini Bowl, Francis Cayouettes, 2014
↑ Butter mould, 1834
→ Lotus enamelware, Grete Prytz Kittelsen and Arne Clausen, Cathrineholm, 1962

↑   Picknick collection, Marianne Westman, Rörstrand, 1954

↑ Stainless-steel dough cutter, Manufactum, 2014

↑ Glass vases, Lyngby Porcelæn, 2015

↑   Flatbread rolling pin
→   Umbrella Stand 115, Wall Shelf 112B, Coat Rack 109C, Pendant Light A110, Mirror 192A, Wall Drawer 114B, Bench 153A, Alvar Aalto, Artek, 1936–52 / Clothes Tree 160, Anna-Maija Jaatinen, 1964; Kanto magazine/firewood rack, Pancho Nikander, 2004

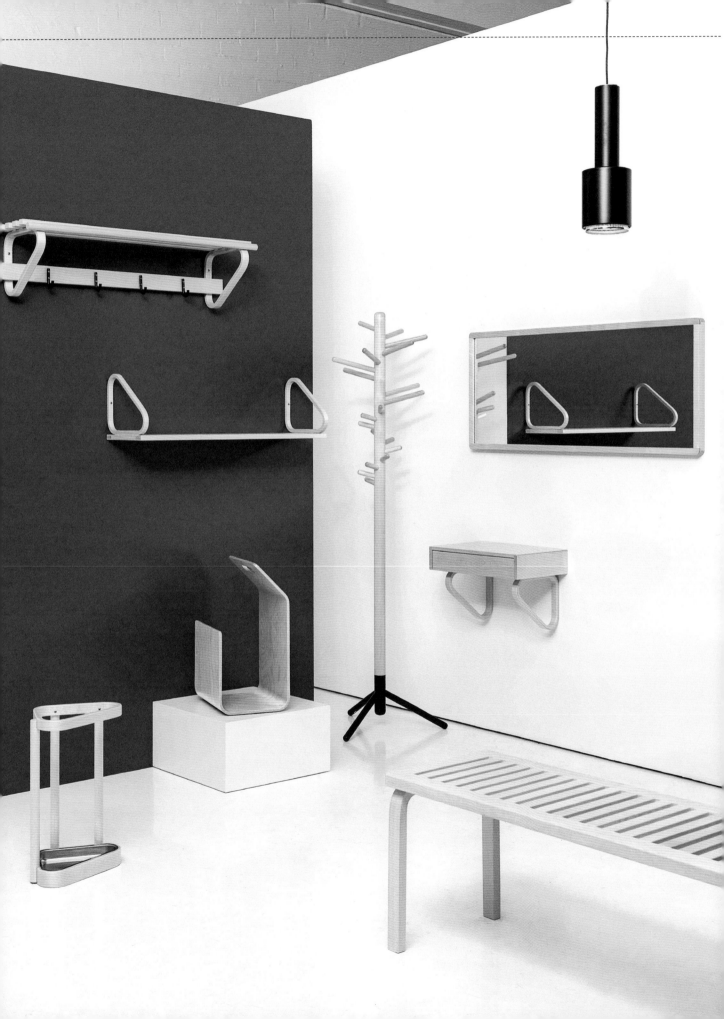

↑　Krenit bowls, Herbert Krenchel, Torben Ørskov, 1953 / Currently manufactured by Normann Copenhagen
→　Sauna stool, Antti Nurmesniemi, G Soderstrom, Helsinki, 1952

↑   Teak Ice Bucket, Jens Quistgaard, Dansk, 1960

↑   Birch-bark wall basket, B Andersson, Hemslöjden, 2014

↑   Variable Balans, Peter Opsvik, Stokke, 1979 / Currently manufactured by Varier Furniture
→   Husqvarna Reliance ice-cream maker, Husqvarna, 1900s

↑   24h Tuokio tableware, Heikki Orvola and Helorinne & Kallio, Arabia, 1996
→   Beolit 500 portable radio, Sigvard Bernadotte and Acton Bjørn, Bang & Olufsen, 1965

-- Design to improve life --

→   Soundwave Swell, Teppo Asikainen, Snowcrash, 1999 / Currently manufactured by Offecct

↑   Reindeer-hide shoes

↑   Candle holder, Arne Jacobsen, Georg Jensen, 1958

↑   Bankers Wall Clock, Arne Jacobsen, Rosendahl, 1971
→   Audio equipment, Jacob Jensen, Bang & Olufsen, 1964–91

↑   Dustpan and Broom, Ole Jensen, Normann Copenhagen, 2002

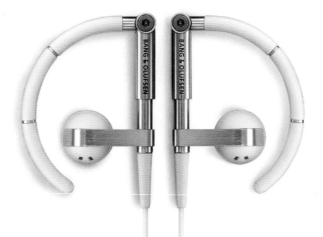

↑ Earset 3i, Anders Hermansen, Bang & Olufsen, 2011

↑   Station Table Clock, Arne Jacobsen, Lauritz Knudsen, 1939 / Currently manufactured by Rosendahl

↑   Sleepi bed, Stokke, 1999

↑   Vipp 15 pedal bin, Holger Nielsen, Vipp, 1939

↑   Butter churner, 1872

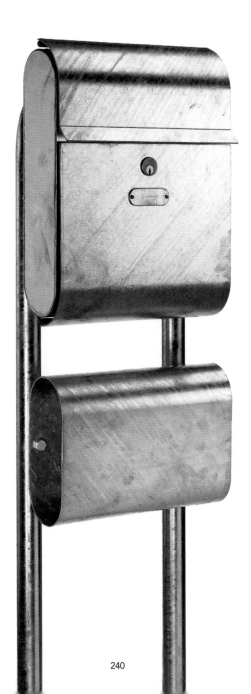

← Danish steel-plate mail box, Manufactum, 2001
↑ Pendel s/10053 lamps, Birger Dahl, Sønnico, 1954 / Currently manufactured by Northern Lighting

↑   Table, Axel Einar Hjorth, Nordiska Kompaniet, 1930

↑   Tati coat rack, Broberg & Ridderstråle, Asplund, 2012

Design to
Improve Relations

Nordic designers are known for their social commitment. This concern became particularly prominent in the twentieth century, when many were intrinsically involved with forging the region's welfare states, designing objects to make everyday life easier, more balanced and more beautiful. The retailers' co-operatives that sprang up in 1940s Denmark were instrumental in popularizing this notion, selling high-quality furniture at a price that was affordable to the general population. Courageously, many saw it as their objective to fix social ills. Seeing design as a process of 'problem solving' has become commonplace in the industry today: but it was architects, designers and indeed even craftsmen from Norway, Denmark, Sweden and Finland who set the precedent for this, long before think tanks and design labs came along.

Design is a tool that Nordic nations use to balance and, importantly, improve society. And there is no better way to understand this philosophy than by looking at their relationship with childhood. In the Nordic region, a child's natural development is wrapped up in a basic belief that all people are created equal. Childhood is, theoretically at least, the ultimate level playing field. Parents tend not to infantilize their young, but instead help them to navigate and understand the world through miniature versions of adult goods. Since the 1960s, design and architecture enthusiasts worldwide have travelled to Denmark to see architect Arne Jacobsen's vision of a modern primary school, in Gentofte near Copenhagen. The school is, quite fantastically, furnished from one end to the other with his extraordinary designs, all at child height.

When the Danish silversmith Kay Bojesen began making toys in the 1920s, he produced them inexpensively using wood from Denmark and Sweden. Some were painted bright blue, red or gold but many were left unpainted because children, according to Bojesen, had enough imagination to bring their own sense of colour to his collection of simple wooden animals and toys [p. 262]. Bojesen drew on his own experiences as a father when he designed toys, but there were other reasons behind his pieces' popularity. He was an early adopter of an approach that characterizes Nordic childhood education and still informs its philosophy today. Nordic people respect children for their own values, for their ability to live in a fantasy world, and are especially respectful of the importance of play. Play is viewed as a fundamental aspect of social development in Nordic countries. While not exclusively concerned with learning, it is understood that if a child is given the time and space to play, he or she will develop valuable emotional, cognitive and physical skills from an early age that will undoubtedly be useful in later life. Which explains why Kay Bojesen's instinct was to create toys not only for a child's enjoyment, but also to stimulate their imagination.

Nordic nations rarely place values on hierarchy, or on class, gender, economic status or age. There is no 'children should be seen and not heard' in this region and that is why, more often than not, you will find Nordic children sharing the dining table with the adults at mealtimes. It is this sense of inclusivity that prompted Danish designer Nanna Ditzel to come up with her ND-08 children's chair [p. 270] in 1955. At the time, she was raising young twin girls and had looked in vain for chairs that were both functional and good-looking enough for them to use at the communal table. Her solution was born, like so many pieces of Nordic furniture, of the designer's own experiences and desire to create something that could benefit ordinary people. The piece has since become a design classic that has shown its functionality and worth over several generations. A similar approach can be seen in Norwegian designer Peter Opsvik's Tripp Trapp high chair [p. 250]. With its deceptively simple structure, which adapts with the child as it grows, it is another strong example of ergonomic and sustainable design, based on democratic values and a desire to problem-solve.

It was no accident that Ditzel and Opsvik chose a dining chair to draw children into the egalitarian family space. 'Sharing' the table is an elemental notion in Nordic nations. Nordic homes reflect this thinking and are designed with the intention to welcome and entertain guests, their open-plan and free-flowing interiors encouraging social interaction at every level. It is no wonder then that one of the most common dining tables in the region is Bruno Mathsson and Piet Heins' Super-Elliptical table [p. 278]. Its ingenious oval shape is a fantastic example of Nordic democratic design as it does not allow for any sort of hierarchy or distance, everyone is afforded an equal position and there is always room for one more.

A common quality in Nordic people is their ability to revel in social openness and display a warm welcome to all. This devotion to entertaining people is probably best witnessed at Christmas. Alongside the Midsummer celebrations, Christmas is arguably the most important occasion of the year. Despite the darkness and winter chill outside – or perhaps because of it – the festive season is when homes are thrown open to family and friends.

Since the old festival of *jól* (from which the word 'yule' is derived), the festive occasion has been a highlight during a very dark season. It is a time when some of the Nordic region's most recognizable symbols come to the fore. Small bales of hay and wooden candlesticks are made into a display that can be traced back to old rural communities. Every year, straw

decorations are hung on the tree and the dining table is set with the family's finest tableware. Lights are placed on windowsills to extend the cheer beyond the domestic realm to people outside too. Christmas is a time of year that is about relationships. It is also a time for giving gifts, and while material possessions are certainly not of equal importance to human interaction, one might argue that good design does have the ability to bring people closer together.

One thing that unites people at Christmas time in the Nordic nations is the shared interest in its diverse heritage of folklore. The great Nordic trope of storytelling binds the Nordic people together, both nationally and regionally. Stretching back to Norse mythology, with its trolls and elves, and the eighteenth-century tales of Hans Christian Andersen, folklore is a huge part of the Nordic tradition. Often these tales and characters take physical form: history and mythology are brought to life as a Dala horse carving [p. 273], a straw Yule goat [p. 261] or a wooden Viking figurine [p. 260]. As popular as the myths and folklore themselves, these mementos can be shared among generations and contribute towards the collective memory of the region. In more ways than one, it is this power of an object to tell a story – a shared story – that makes design so important in this part of the world, at any time of year.

↑ Rocking Horse, Kay Bojesen, Kay Bojesen Denmark, 1936
→ CH411 and CH410 (Peter's Table and Chair), Hans Wegner, Carl Hansen & Søn, 1944 / Wooden toys, Kay Bojesen, Kay Bojesen Denmark, 1930–57

↑   Tripp Trapp high chair, Peter Opsvik, Stokke, 1972

↑   Arch:You oak figurines, Anne Boysen, Applicata, 2010

↑   Model 304 drop-leaf dining table, Niels Kofoed, Kofoed Møbelfabrik, 1964

↑   Child's Chair, Kristian Vedel, Torben Ørskov, 1957 / Currently manufactured by Architectmade

↑   Puffin, Kay Bojesen, Kay Bojesen Denmark, 1954
→   Dachshund, Brio, 1958

↑   Turned, Lars Beller Fjetland, Hem, 2013

HET VERZAMELD
BEDRIJVEN

← Streamliner Classic toy car, Ulf Hanses, Samhall, 1984 / Currently manufactured by Playsam
↑ Royal Life Guard, Kay Bojesen, Kay Bojesen Denmark, 1942

↑   Wood figure, Arne Tjomsland, Goodwill, 1957
→   Straw goats

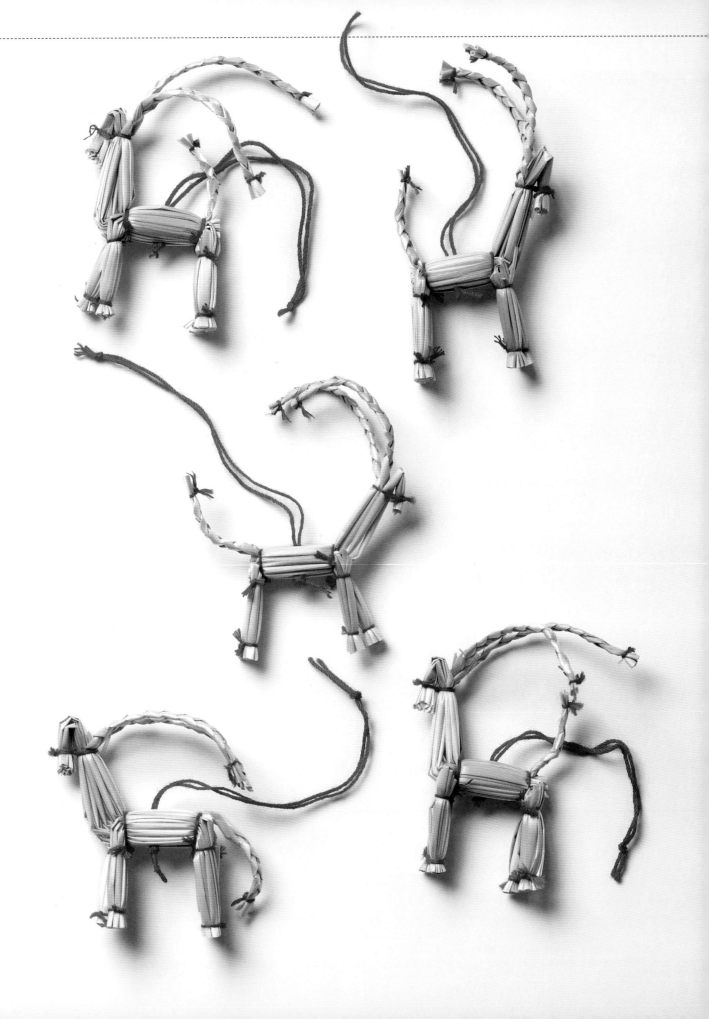

↑   Wooden toy collection, Kay Bojesen, Kay Bojesen Denmark, 1930–57
→   Lego bricks, Lego, 1958

↑   Mammut children's chair, Ikea, 1994
→   Vippelhøne (Crazy Hen), Tom Lindhardt, Kompan, 1971
↠   Office collection, Hay, 2013

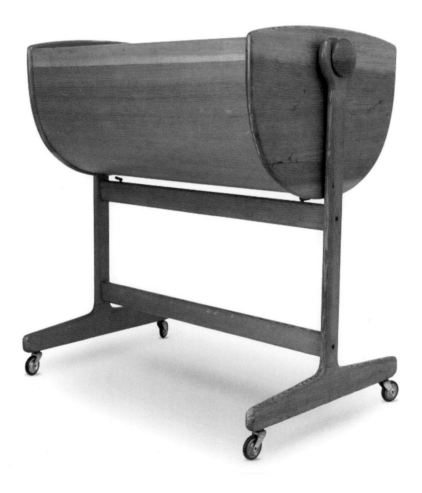

↑ Lulu Cradle, Nanna Ditzel, Poul Kold, 1963 / Currently manufactured by Brdr. Krüger
→ Puppy, Eero Aarnio, Magis, 2005

↑   Elephant Party 71 Mobile, Ole Flensted, Flensted Mobiles, 1976

↑   A la Carte ceramic collection, Hermann Bongard, Figgjo, c.1959

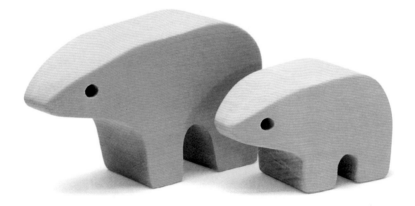

↑   Polar Bears, Ole Søndergaard, Osgrafik, 2012
→   Untitled paper cutting, Hans Christian Andersen, 1864

↑   Tea Trollies, Tapio Wirkkala, Asko, 1940s

↑   Children's Furniture, Alvar Aalto, 1940s

↑   Super-Elliptical table, Piet Hein and Bruno Mathsson, Fritz Hansen, 1964

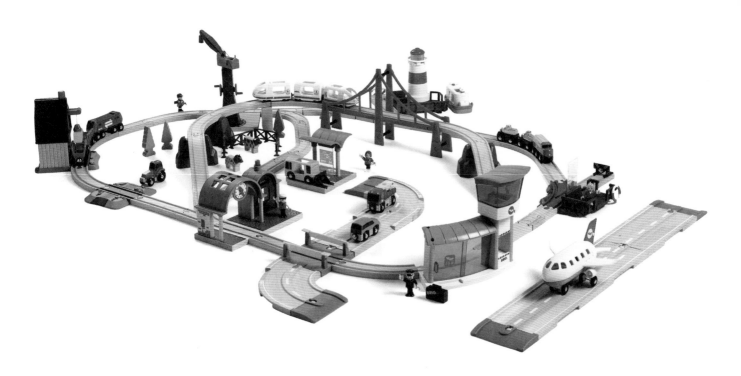

↑ Train Set, Brio, 1957

Index

Page numbers in *italics* refer to illustrations

Picture Credits

1stdibs 23, 119, 121, 124, 182-3, 252; &Tradition 64, 80, 98; Adelta 133; AEO Studio, photo by Daniella Witte 22; AGA Rangemaster Ltd., 171; agefotostock, photo by Lisa Wahman 117; American Swedish Institute, Minneapolis, Minnesota 190, 193, 200, 212, 218, 230, 239, 273; Anderssen & Voll 195; © Arabia/Fiskars Group 122–3, 226; Architectmade 63, 67, 253; © ARTEK 16, 26, 30, 31, 42, 104, 127, 139, 143 (image courtesy Jackson Design - jacksons.se), 149 (Artek 2nd cycle), 219; Asko, image courtesy Jackson Design - jacksons.se 276; Asplund, photo by Louise Bilgert 243; Bang & Olufsen 47 (photo by Jesper Jørgen), 227, 235; Bemz, image courtesy Jackson Design - jacksons.se 126; Bodum 187; Anne Boysen 251; Brdr. Krüger 68, 268 (image courtesy 1stdibs); © BRIO AB 255, 279; © Bruno Mathsson International AB 88; © by Lassen 36, 79, 95; Carl Hansen & Søn 35, 62, 77, 105 (photo by Jessica Bruah), 249; DACS 2016, image courtesy Phillips 191, Dansk/Lenox Group 157 (image courtesy 1stdibs), 159, 188–9, 222 (image courtesy 1stdibs); Design by Us, photo by Line Thit Klein, styling by Nathalie Schwer 131; Design Forum Finland 221; Design House Stockholm 48, 168; Design Museum Denmark, photo by Pernille Klemp 100; © dk3 34, 90–91; Engelbrechts 81; Erik Jørgensen 32–33, 52; © Fiskars Group 154; Flensted Mobiles 271; © Fredericia Furniture A/S 29, 54; © Hackman/Fiskars Group 153; Hans Christian Andersen Museum, Odense, Denmark 275; Fine Little Day 223; © Finlandia Sauna Products, Inc., photo by Todd Eckelman Photography 206; Fjordfiesta, photo by Espen Istad 103; Freight Shop Ltd. 27; Fritz Hansen A/S 16, 20, 21, 24, 36, 39, 40, 45, 76, 141, 278; © Gense 164; Georg Jensen 107, 210, 231; GUBI 74,140; Gurli Elbækgaard 60; Habitek, image courtesy Jackson Design - jacksons.se 135; © HAY 266–7; © Hem 256–7; Holmegaard/ Rosendahl Design Group 28; © Iittala/Fiskars Group 50, 51, 65, 83, 92, 99, 110 (image courtesy Jackson Design - jacksons.se), 112, 148, 153, 167, 170, 172, 179, 207 (image courtesy Connox); © Inter IKEA Systems B.V. 43, 202, 264; Jackson Design - jacksons.se 277; © Jacob Jensen Design A/S 233; KH Würtz, photo by Gentl and Hyers 108–9; Kay Bojesen Denmark/Rosendahl Design Group A/S 248, 254, 259, 262; Kiosk 176, 192, 194; KOMPAN 265; Kvadrat 38; © Lange Production ApS 49; LE KLINT 55; Lego 263; © Les Arts Décoratifs, Paris/Jean Tholance/akg-images 177; Ligne Roset 158; Louis Poulsen & Co. 44, 85, 94; Lyngby Porcelæn/ Rosendahl Design Group A/S 150, 217; Magis, photo by Max Rommel 269; Manufactum 114, 216, 240; Marimekko 155, 173; Marta Maas Fjetterström, image courtesy 1stdibs 142; Mater 61; Mjolk, photo by Blaise Misiek 174; Montana 115; Museum of Design in Plastics, Arts University Bournemouth 180; © 2016. Digital image, The Museum of Modern Art, New York/Scala, Florence 201; Museum Southeast Denmark, photo by Jens Olsen 185; Muuto 69, 156, 165, 205; Nanna Ditzel Design A/S, photo by Erik Hansen 270; The National Museum of Art, Architecture and Design, Norway 46 (photo by Andreas Harvik), 116; Nordiska Kompaniet, image courtesy Jackson Design - jacksons.se 137, 242; Normann Copenhagen 181, 220, 234; Norwegian Icons 53, 102, 113, 118, 125, 130, 178, 184, 213, 241, 260, 272; OeO Studio 19; Offecct 229; Erik Olsson 224; Onecollection A/S 72, 73, 78, 82; Orrefors 58, 86, 96 (image courtesy 1stdibs), 134 (image courtesy Jackson Design - jacksons.se), 136 (image courtesy of Kultur-parken Småland AB); PP Møbler 75, 93, 106, 111, 129; © Peter Opsvik AS 224, 250; Phillips 128; Playsam, photo by Linda Lindström 258; © Pia Wallén 228; © Raadvad/Fiskars Group 163, 186; Robert Matton AB/Alamy Stock Photo 261; Rosendahl Design Group A/S 232, 236; Rosenthal GmbH 132; Rosti Mepal 198–9; © Rörstrand/Fiskars Group 175 (image courtesy National Museum of Art and Design, Sweden), 214–15 (image courtesy Bukowskis); © Royal Copenhagen/Fiskars Group 151, 196, 208 (image courtesy 1stdibs); Russell & George, Stepped House, photo by Dianna Snape 41; Sika Design 57; © Skagerak A/S 18, 25; Skultuna 66, 203; Sløjd, photo by Seidel Photography 197; Ole Søndergaard 274; © Stelton A/S 160–61, 169, 204, 211; © Stig Lindberg/DACS 2016, image courtesy Junichi Kabusaki 209; Stokke® 237; StokkeAustad 87, 97; Stolab Möbel 100; Svenskt Tenn 84; Swedish Rags 56; Tortus Copenhagen 89; © VENINI S.p.A., image courtesy Aldo Ballo 58; Vipp 238; Vitra 138; Vola 162; We Do Wood 120; Zilencio 166

Every reasonable effort has been made to acknowledge the ownership of copyright for photographs included in this volume. Any errors that may have occurred are inadvertent, and will be corrected in subsequent editions provided notification is sent in writing to the publisher.

Phaidon Press Limited
Regent's Wharf
All Saints Street
London N1 9PA

Phaidon Press Inc.
65 Bleecker Street
New York, NY 10012

phaidon.com

First Published in 2017
© 2017 Phaidon Press Limited

ISBN 978 0 7148 7347 3

A CIP catalogue record for this book is available from the British Library and the Library of Congress.

Commissioning Editor: Emilia Terragni
Project Editor: Robyn Taylor
Production Controller: Adela Cory
Design: Oak Publishing

Printed in China

The publisher would like to thank the American Swedish Institute, Minneapolis, Minnesota, Sarah Bell and Tom Morris for their contributions to the book.

The author would like to thank Lars Hedebo, Julie Vitto and Lise Ulrich.

Editor's note: images that do not list a designer, manufacturer or date are representative of traditional, anonymously-designed objects from the Nordic region, for which such factual details are not applicable.